To:

From:

Cats
Are Special

GRAMERCY BOOKS
NEW YORK

Published by Gramercy Books, an imprint of Random House Value Publishing, a division of Random House, Inc., New York.

Gramercy is a registered trademark and the colophon is a trademark of Random House, Inc.

Random House
New York • Toronto • London • Sydney • Auckland
www.randomhouse.com

Compiled by Kira Baum
Interior design by Christine Kell

Printed and bound in China

Library of Congress Cataloging-in-Publication Data

Cats Are Special : a tribute to elegance, playfulness, and grace.
   p. cm.
   ISBN: 978-0-517-22882-1
   1. Cats—Quotations, maxims, etc. 2. Cats—Pictorial works.

PN6084.C23C36 2007
636.8—dc22

                                                    2006044438

10 9 8 7 6 5 4 3 2 1

Acknowledgments: 1, *Pixtal/Superstock.* 3, *Martin Bydalek/UpperCut Images.* 5, *Pixtal/Superstock.* 7, *Ron Chapple/Thinkstock/Superstock.* 9, *Martin Bydalek/UpperCut Images.* 11, *PhotoAlto/Punchstock.* 12-13, *Pixtal/Superstock.* 14, *Brian Hamilton/Alamy.* 17, *Don Mason/Brand X Pictures/PictureQuest.* 19, *Photo 24/Brand X Pictures/PictureQuest.* 21, *Juniors Bildarchiv/Alamy.* 22, *Medioimages/Punchstock.* 24-25, *Pixtal/Superstock.* 27, *PhotoAlto/Superstock.* 29, *Corbis.* 31, *Masterfile.* 32-33, *Brand X Pictures/Punchstock.* 34, *Photodisc/Punchstock.* 37, *Pixtal/Superstock.* 39, *Vladimir Godnik/Alamy.* 40-41, *Pixtal/Superstock.* 43, *Walter Geiersperger/Index Stock.* 44, *Thinkstock/Punchstock.* 47, *Corbis.* 49, *Brand X Pictures/Punchstock.* 50-51, *Pixtal/Superstock.* 53, *Pixtal/Superstock.* 55, *Corbis.* 56, *Corbis.* 58-59, *Pixtal/Superstock.* 61, *Pixtal/Superstock.* 63, *Pam Mitsakos.* 64, *Brand X Pictures/Punchstock.*

Cats
Are Special

To err is human, to purr feline.

ROBERT BYRNE

Cat people are different, to the extent that they generally are not conformists. How could they be, with a cat running their lives?

LOUIS CAMUTI

A happy arrangement: many people prefer cats to other people, and many cats prefer people to other cats.

MASON COOLEY

Don't waste your money on professional psychiatric fees for your cat. You will need it for your own analysis.

STEPHEN BAKER, *How to Live With a Neurotic Cat*

There is, incidentally, no way of talking about cats that enables one to come off as a sane person.

DAN GREENBERG

He marveled at the fact that cats had two holes cut in their
fur at precisely the spot where their eyes were.

GEORG CHRISTOPH LICHTENBERG

I got rid of my husband. The cat was allergic.

UNKNOWN

By associating with the cat one only risks becoming richer.

SIDONIE GABRIELLE

Authors like cats because they are such quiet, lovable, wise creatures,
and cats like authors for the same reasons.

ROBERTSON DAVIES

Perhaps it is because cats do not live by human patterns,
do not fit themselves into prescribed behavior,
that they are so united to creative people.

ANDRE NORTON

"I didn't know that Cheshire cats always grinned;
in fact, I didn't know that cats *could* grin."
"They all can," said the Duchess; "and most of 'em do."
"I don't know of any that do," Alice said very politely, feeling quite
pleased to have got into a conversation.
"You don't know much," said the Duchess; "and that's a fact."

LEWIS CARROLL, *Alice's Adventures in Wonderland*

I love cats because I enjoy my home; and little by little,
they become its visible soul.

JEAN COCTEAU

A house without a cat, and a well-fed, well-petted and
properly revered cat, may be a perfect home, perhaps,
but how can it prove its title?

MARK TWAIN

One small cat changes coming home to an
empty house to coming home.

PAM BROWN

It is difficult to obtain the friendship of a cat. It is a philosophical
animal...one that does not place its affections thoughtlessly.

THEOPHILE GAUTIER

It's funny how dogs and cats know the inside of folks better
than other folks do, isn't it?

ELEANOR H. PORTER, *Pollyanna*

In nine lifetimes, you'll never know as much about
your cat as your cat knows about you.

MICHEL DE MONTAIGNE

I have studied many philosophers and many cats.
The wisdom of cats is infinitely superior.

HIPPOLYTTE TAINE

Beware of people who dislike cats.

IRISH SAYING

People who hate cats will come back as mice in their next life.

UNKNOWN

When your cat rubs the side of its face along your leg,
it's affectionately marking you with its scent, identifying you as
its private property, saying, in effect, "You belong to me."

SUSAN MCDONOUGH

I had been told that the training procedure with cats was difficult.
It's not. Mine had me trained in two days.

BILL DANA

Life with a cat is in certain ways a one-sided proposition.
Cats are not educable; humans are. Moreover, cats know this. If you're
not willing to humor them, you might as well stick to dogs.

TERRY TEACHOUT

When I play with my cat, who knows if I am not a pastime
to her more than she is to me.

MONTAIGNE

Cats always know whether people like or dislike them.
They do not always care enough to do anything about it.

WINIFRED CARRIERE

As anyone who has ever been around a cat for any length of time knows,
cats have enormous patience with the limitations of the human kind.

CLEVELAND AMORY

Cats regard people as warmblooded furniture.

JACQUELYN MITCHARD, *The Deep End of the Ocean*

A cat can maintain a position of curled-up somnolence on your
knee until you are nearly upright. To the last minute she hopes your
conscience will get the better of you and you will settle down again.

PAM BROWN

For me, one of the pleasures of cats' company is
their devotion to bodily comfort.

COMPTON MACKENZIE, SR.

Time spent with cats is never wasted.

SIGMUND FREUD

There is something about the presence of a cat...that
seems to take the bite out of being alone.

LOUIS CAMUTI

A cat will be your friend, but never your slave.

THEOPHILE GAUTIER

O heaven will not ever heaven be
Unless my cats are there to welcome me.

EPITAPH IN A PET CEMETERY

[My cat] George Eliot was given to me as a Christmas
present by a Norwegian friend of mine who, cribbing a line
from an I.J. Fox ad, observed that "a small fur piece is a
joy forever"....We established an immediate rapport and while
we have had our ups and downs, we have, on the whole,
been much contented with each other for seven years.

JEAN STAFFORD, "George Eliot: A Medical Study"

FROM "ON THE DEATH OF A CAT, A FRIEND OF MINE, AGED TEN YEARS AND A HALF"

Who shall tell the lady's grief
When her Cat was past relief?
Who shall number the hot tears
Shed o'er her, beloved for years?
Who shall say the dark dismay
Which her dying caused that day?

CHRISTINA ROSSETTI

Cats are magical...the more you pet them the longer you both live.

ANONYMOUS

There is, indeed, no single quality of the cat that
man could not emulate to his advantage.

CARL VAN VECHTEN

If man could be crossed with the cat, it would
improve man but deteriorate the cat.

MARK TWAIN

Cat-lovers will no doubt point out that the elegance and dignity of
cats are the consequence of their sojourn in the temples of the
gods, where their attitudes and movements were regarded as
divine prognostications. Be that as it may, it is obvious that the
cat's wealth of expressions makes it an ideal candidate for such a
role. Unlike the dog, which either wags its tail or does not wag its
tail, the cat possesses a wide range of means to convey its
emotions: It arches its back, makes its fur stand on end, meows,
rubs itself against furniture and against humans, purrs, lashes its
tail, spits, and hisses. The priests of Bacht, therefore, had ample
material for interpretation.

PHILIPPE DIOLÉ

God made the cat that man might have the pleasure of caressing the tiger.

FERDINAND MERY

For what lady in all the world could say "no" to the passionate
yet *toujours* discreet advances of a fine marmalade cat?

ANGELA CARTER, "Puss-in-Boots"

There are two means of refuge from the
miseries of life: music and cats.

ALBERT SCHWEITZER

A cat is never vulgar.

CARL VAN VECHTEN

With the qualities of cleanliness, affection, patience,
dignity, and courage that cats have, how many of us, I ask you,
would be capable of becoming cats?

FERDINAND MERY

A meow massages the heart.

STUART MCMILLAN

If we treated everyone we meet with the same affection we
bestow upon our favorite cat, they, too, would purr.

MARTIN BUXBAUM

If cats could talk, they wouldn't.

NAN PORTER

A cat determined not to be found can fold itself up like a
pocket handkerchief if it wants to.

LOUIS CAMUTI

Cats are no bother at all. As long as you feed them right,
let them sleep in your bed, scratch their back at their
convenience, give them enough room on the living room
couch, play with them when they want to, talk to them at
length, and spend every waking hour (theirs) with them.

STEPHEN BAKER, *How to Live With a Neurotic Cat*

Lettin' the cat outta the bag is
a whole lot easier 'n puttin' it back in.

WILL ROGERS

Who among us hasn't envied a cat's ability to ignore
the cares of daily life and to relax completely?

KAREN BRADEMEYER

As every cat owner knows, nobody owns a cat.

ELLEN PERRY BERKELEY

The cat is a dilettante in fur.

THEOPHILE GAUTIER

Cats have it all—admiration, an endless sleep,
and company only when they want it.

ROD MCKUEN

Cats are autocrats of naked self-interest. They are both amoral and immoral, consciously breaking rules. Their "evil" look at such times is no human projection: the cat may be the only animal who savors the perverse or reflects upon it.

CAMILLE PAGLIA

Cats seem to go on the principle that it never does any harm to ask for what you want.

JOSEPH WOOD KRUTCH

Cats are inquisitive, but hate to admit it.

MASON COOLEY

After scolding one's cat one looks into its face and is seized by the ugly suspicion that it understood every word. And has filed it for reference.

CHARLOTTE GRAY

Some people say that cats are sneaky, evil, and cruel. True,
and they have many other fine qualities as well.

MISSY DIZICK

Cats are kindly masters, just so long as you remember your place.

PAUL GRAY

The Naming of Cats is a difficult matter,
It isn't just one of your holiday games;
You may think at first I'm as mad as a hatter
When I tell you, a cat must have THREE DIFFERENT NAMES.

T.S. ELIOT, *Old Possum's Book of Practical Cats*

Anyone who considers protocol unimportant
has never dealt with a cat.

ROBERT A. HEINLEIN

With Cats, some say, one rule is true:
Don't speak till you are spoken to.
Myself, I do not hold with that—
I say, you should ad-dress a Cat.
But always keep in mind that he
Resents familiarity.
I bow, and taking off my hat,
Ad-dress him in this form: O CAT!

T.S. ELIOT, *Old Possum's Book of Practical Cats*

There is no snooze button on a cat who wants breakfast.

ANONYMOUS

All I do is eat and sleep. Eat and sleep. Eat and sleep.
There must be more to a cat's life than that. But I hope not.

GARFIELD, CREATED BY JIM DAVIS

Cats like canned food, cheap, wet, disgusting, canned food. Who can blame them? How many of us, while eating a bacon and egg sandwich on soft white bread with butter, say to ourselves, "This food is not good for me at any stage of life," and then go on blissfully stuffing those savory bites into our mouths? Why expect your cat to be more restrained than you are?

NICOLE HOLLANDER, *Cats With Attitude*

Cats are connoisseurs of comfort.

JAMES HERRIOT

If there is one spot of sun spilling onto the floor,
a cat will find it and soak it up.

UNKNOWN

A cat pours his body on the floor like water.
It is restful just to see him.

WILLIAM LYON PHELPS

Kittens are born with their eyes shut. They open them
in about six days, take a look around, then close them again
for the better part of their natural lives.

STEPHEN BAKER, *How to Live with a Neurotic Cat*

Grooming your cat is an activity pleasurable to both cat and owner.
Your cat purrs while you hum Sinatra tunes to yourself. It's a lovely
moment; don't ruin it by deciding to plait her fur into little braids
all over her body and tying off the ends with tiny magenta ribbons.

NICOLE HOLLANDER, *Cats With Attitude*

Balanchine has trained his cat to perform brilliant *jetés* and *tours en l'air*;
he says that at last he has a body worth choreographing for.

BERNARD TAPER

Women and cats will do as they please, and men and dogs
should relax and get used to the idea.

ROBERT A. HEINLEIN

Cats exercise ... a magic influence upon highly developed men of intellect. This is why these long-tailed Graces of the animal kingdom, these adorable, scintillating electric batteries have been the favorite animal of a Mohammed, Cardinal Richlieu, Crebillon, Rousseau, Wieland.

LEOPOLD VON SACHER-MASOCH

Watch a cat when it enters a room for the first time. It searches and smells about, it is not quiet for a moment, it trusts nothing until it has examined and made acquaintance with everything.

JEAN-JACQUES ROUSSEAU

[A cat is] the emblem of restlessness and impatience at the same moment. A restless cat no more remains in the same place than a silk thread does which is wafted idly to and fro with every breath of air. A cat on the watch is as motionless as death stationed at its place of observation, and neither hunger nor thirst can possibly draw it away from its meditation.

ALEXANDRE DUMAS, *The Three Musketeers*

Cats are smarter than dogs. You can't get eight cats to
pull a sled through snow.

JEFF VALDEZ

Every dog has his day—but the nights are reserved for the cats.

ANONYMOUS

The dog may be wonderful prose, but only the cat is poetry.

FRENCH PROVERB

It's easy to understand why the cat has eclipsed the dog as modern
America's favorite pet. People like pets to possess the same qualities they
do. Cats are irresponsible and recognize no authority, yet are completely
dependent on others for their material needs. Cats cannot be made to do
anything useful. Cats are mean for the fun of it.

P. J. O'ROURKE

A show of disdain has long been a favorite ploy of cats. It clearly sets them apart from their major competitors, dogs, whose obsequious manners cats consider not only unbecoming but a complete waste of energy and time.

STEPHEN BAKER, *5001 Names for Cats*

Dogs believe they are human. Cats believe they are God.

UNKNOWN

Dogs come when they're called;
cats take a message and get back to you later.

MARY BLY

Dogs have Owners, Cats have Staff!

ANONYMOUS

If animals could speak, the dog would be a blundering outspoken fellow;
but the cat would have the rare grace of never saying a word too much.

MARK TWAIN

Cats seldom waste words. They are quiet beasts. They keep their counsel, they reflect. They reflect all day, and at night their eyes reflect.

URSULA K. LE GUIN, "Schrödinger's Cat"

The cat has too much spirit to have no heart.

ERNEST MENAUL

A cat has nine lives.

THOMAS FULLER

It's better to feed one cat than many mice.

NORWEGIAN PROVERB

A kitten is in the animal world what a rosebud is in a garden.

ROBERT SOUTHEY

No matter how much cats fight,
there always seem to be plenty of kittens.

ABRAHAM LINCOLN

A cat is a puzzle for which there is no solution.

HAZEL NICHOLSON

He will kill mice, and he will be kind to Babies when he is in the house,
just as long as they do not pull his tail too hard. But when he has done
that, and between times, and when the moon gets up and night comes,
he is the Cat that walks by himself, and all places are alike to him.

RUDYARD KIPLING, "The Cat that Walked by Himself"

"All right," said the Cat; and this time it
vanished quite slowly, beginning with the end of the
tail and ending with the grin, which remained some
time after the rest of it had gone.

"Well! I've often seen a cat without a grin,"
thought Alice, "but a grin without a cat! It's the most
curious thing I ever saw in all my life!"

LEWIS CARROLL, *Alice's Adventures in Wonderland*